To Stephanie

CW00393408

SEIKO

The story of a Japanese girl

OLGA ABRAHAMS

illustrations by John Rawding

OMF BOOKS

© OVERSEAS MISSIONARY FELLOWSHIP

First published	...	...	*September 1973*
Revised edition	...	...	*June 1976*
Reprinted ...	...	...	*January 1980*

ISBN 0 85363 112 3

*Published by the Overseas Missionary Fellowship
Belmont, The Vine, Sevenoaks, Kent TN13 3TZ
and printed by
Stanley L. Hunt (Printers) Ltd.
Midland Road, Rushden, Northants*

CONTENTS

CHAPTER ONE

A NEW HOME

GRANDFATHER's hotel was alive with excitement. The maids had swept the *tatami* matting in the rooms and washed the old wooden floors of the corridors and entrance. It looked as though the boards had a thick wax finish, but the rich deep polish was just the result of years of constant washing. The charcoal in the brazier glowed a welcoming red; steam rose steadily from the gleaming brass kettle. Everything was ready for the important guest.

The hotel was one of the most important in the island of Sakhalin near the northern end of the great Japanese Empire. My grandfather was a leading man in the town of Toro, and as a result of his hard work and constant activity he was pretty well off. His family were grown up. His first wife had died, and now his second wife was helping him to run the hotel.

'She's come!' the word flew around, and a strange shuffling sound could be heard as the maids glided along the polished floors in their slippers. Grandfather and his wife both hurried to the entrance; and now the maids were on their knees to greet the visitors. The front door slid open with a grating noise and a puff of cold air, and in came a gentleman with something on his back. Everyone knelt down and bowed politely in greeting. The maids helped him to take off his coat, and there underneath was a red bundle. He took off his long boots and put on the heelless slippers they offered him.

Once more bows were exchanged.

'We are glad you have arrived safely,' Grandfather greeted him.

'It's a long time since I saw you, Father,' the visitor replied. 'I hope you are as well as usual.'

He untied the cords of the bundle on his back, and Grandmother gently lifted it down and held it lovingly in her arms. The important guest they had been waiting for, the bundle itself, was me, just a baby of about a year and a half! I was coming not just for a visit, but to stay. I peeped out of the top of the thick wadded red kimono, and looked round at the strange friendly faces. Grandmother removed the kimono so that I could toddle around. I smiled happily as she fondled and fussed over me. I was too young to understand the troubles my family were having. My own mother, expecting another baby, was too weak to look after all my brothers and sisters, so I was to have new parents—my grandfather and his childless second wife. Grandmother was specially pleased to have a baby of her own. She joyfully took me off to the living room where I was the centre of attention from half a dozen maids. Grandfather led my father solemnly into the special guest room to hold a longer and more serious conversation.

In the centre of the guest room was a beautiful lacquered table about a foot high. Square cushions were arranged round it. The room was square, but in one corner there was a recess with a large scroll hanging in it. Flowers had been carefully arranged and placed below the scroll. Next to the recess was the only other piece of furniture in the room, which looked like a decorated lacquer cupboard. It was the god-shelf. Fresh flowers and fruit were placed in front of it. Above was a picture of my real grandmother and inside the cupboard a white board on which her name was written. This was not the name she had

always had but the name the priest gave her when she died.

The doors of the god-shelf were usually kept closed, but today they were wide open. As my father and grandfather entered the room they slipped off their shoes, knelt down and bowed low before the god-shelf. They were to have an important conversation, so they wanted the spirits of their ancestors to join in too.

Then they sat down at the table. The maids brought in green tea and sweet sticky cakes and withdrew very quietly and respectfully, sliding the doors shut behind them. Grandfather and Father were left alone in the presence of the spirits of the dead.

'Thank you very much for taking our miserable daughter off our hands, Father. I'm afraid she will be nothing but trouble to you,' said my father.

'Not at all,' answered the older man. 'We are very pleased to have a baby in the family again. My wife is specially pleased. But how is Seiko's* mother?'

'Thank you for your concern—I'm afraid she is very weak. The doctor is worried that her heart won't be able to stand the strain of having the baby. Four children are a bit of a handful. We're thankful that the other three are well and growing up, and now Seiko has a good home her mother will be much relieved.'

After that father and son remained in deep conversation for a long time. When it was time to leave, my father peeped in to see me playing happily with my new friends. From that day I would cease to be his daughter. He said goodbye cheerfully, and only as he set off in the snow again for his own home did he allow the tears he had felt in his heart to well up in his eyes.

For me a new life had begun.

---

* Seiko is pronounced 'Say Co'.

CHAPTER TWO

SHELTER

It didn't take me long to settle down in my new home. Everybody loved me. I toddled about the hotel, made friends with the maids and became specially fond of my grandfather and grandmother, who would do anything for me.

I never saw my baby sister; she only lived a few days. My mother, weakened and distressed, died a little later, but I can't remember the funeral. Soon after this war came. Father, who had married again, joined the army, and my brothers and sisters were looked after by his new wife. I was lucky because Grandfather was already looking after me. Throughout Japan food got scarcer and scarcer. People were afraid of bombs, but here in the far north I had plenty to eat, lots of clothes and a warm house to live in. Grandfather was an important man so many people brought him gifts.

I loved visitors coming to the hotel, and I used to run along to the porch to find out who had arrived. When Uncle came he would lift me up in his arms.

'Come in and play with me!' I begged.

He would smile and come slowly along the corridor. He was too ill and frail to work—that was why he came so often. He put his handkerchief across my face: 'Where is she? Where is she? Where is she?' 'Oh! There she is!' he pulled the handkerchief away and we both laughed happily together. Grandmother went along to the kitchen to get him something to eat.

'I wonder how safe it is for him to be playing with the child?' she thought to herself. 'I hope she doesn't catch this terrible lung disease.' Uncle had tuberculosis

very badly. 'Still, it's not for very long. He does love Seiko so much—she's his one and only enjoyment in life.' She shrugged her shoulders and went on preparing the meal.

'This is delicious. Thank you very much,' said Uncle, enjoying the dish of rice with mushrooms, egg and chicken that Grandmother had made. He looked at me. I'd had my dinner so I was just sitting there watching him. The chicken was specially tasty so he chewed on it to make it more tender and, as a special favour, popped it into my mouth. Quite unaware of any danger, I enjoyed it too. Grandmother was horrified. She was quite used to the custom of passing on a tasty bit to a favourite child—but this was different. Uncle was a sick man. Still, she didn't want to spoil his pleasure, and again she just hoped for the best, not saying a word.

That was one of Uncle's last visits. Nobody told me when he died. I just wondered why he didn't come and play with me any more.

CHAPTER THREE

THE BLACK VEIL

ALTHOUGH I was still very small, I remember like a nightmare the next things that happened to me. Although Uncle didn't come to play with me, I ran around the house from one friendly person to the next. I liked meeting people, and I loved company. Grandfather was usually busy, but when he had time I sat on his knee, and that was the best place of all. Then I started to stumble. My legs seemed stiff. I couldn't run about the way I wanted to, and I couldn't see properly—everything was getting blurred, and day by day it became darker and darker. Some days I could hardly move.

My grandparents noticed the change and realized that I was sick, though they didn't know what was the matter.

'What ought we to do?' asked Grandfather. 'There aren't any good hospitals on Sakhalin.'

'We can't take her to the mainland,' replied Grandmother. 'With the war on we'd probably be bombed or the ship would be sunk on the way.'

'You'd better take her to the city hospital here,' Grandfather said. 'We must get her to a doctor quickly.'

Grandmother clapped her hands and bowed in front of the god-shelf. She made sure that the spirits had enough food, and that she was looking after them in the right way. She asked them to help her at the hospital and to make little Seiko better. They were the only gods she knew—the messengers of Christ had reached Sakhalin, but only a few of the people there had believed in Him. Looking back, I can see that the true God was looking after me although we didn't know Him.

Grandmother strapped me on her back, put a large shawl over us both and set out for the hospital. I enjoyed the trip, although I knew she was worried and I couldn't see too well. The hospital was a cold-looking, grey building. Strange people in white over-alls walked quietly about, and there were smells I didn't recognize. We waited for a long time on wooden benches in a very hot room, where nurses kept adding wood to the burning stove. At last Grand-mother's name was called, and then I began to get frightened. They took off my clothes; the doctor felt all over me and stuck needles into me, hurting me. Then he spoke seriously to Grandmother.

'Has the child had contact with tuberculosis?' he asked.

'Yes,' replied Grandmother. 'Her uncle recently died from the disease.'

How vividly she remembered the way Uncle had played with me and given me food from his own mouth! She didn't dare tell the doctor that.

The doctor looked grave. 'This sickness is caused by the same germ,' he explained. 'I hope we have caught it in time. Seiko must stay in hospital. If the disease goes much further she will die.'

The nurse led us to a room with a lot of beds in it. I had never slept in a bed before; I had always been on my mattress on the floor, and usually with Grand-mother. She explained that I would have to stay there until I was better, and I couldn't go back to Grand-father just now. She told me there would always be someone with me.

The doctor was very clever, but the disease had

affected the bones in my neck, and that's why I have this funny neck, which is so short and stiff even today. But the worst part was my eyes. Light got in even when I closed them, so for a long time I had to wear a horrible black veil. I hated it. The hospital was a nice clean place, though, and Grandmother was with me most of the time, sleeping at night on a mattress on the floor.

At last I was allowed out of the hospital, but I still had to wear that horrible black veil, especially in the snow. My body was cured, but the veil that shielded my eyes from the sunshine kept me in. When at last it was removed, I still felt that my life would always be dark. I couldn't move my head freely, I didn't want to talk to anybody, smile at anybody, or play with anybody. I liked to be with my grandparents, but I avoided nearly everybody else. I played a little with some Russian and Korean children, and I remember having a wonderful time when Grandfather took me out on his sledge. But mostly everything was dark and dreary. I almost wished I hadn't gone to hospital; then I could have died.

CHAPTER FOUR

RUSSIAN BOOTS

BACK home again, everything was different, and everyone seemed to be against me. I refused to do anything I was told. One day when I was outside, playing with my Korean friends, a huge Russian dog chased me and I ran out into the house terrified. I didn't want to stay in, and I didn't want to go out except when Grandfather took me on his big sledge.

Everyone in the hotel seemed different too. They looked worried, and moved very quietly. I noticed that there were many discussions in the little room with the god-shelf doors wide open. There must be something very important going on if the ancestors—and I suppose my mother was among them now—had to be told about it all the time. Grandmother made sure they had enough; every morning I joined her as we clapped our hands and put the water and rice out for them at the god-shelf.

And then one day I heard the noise of tramping in the street—Russian soldiers had entered our town. They made full use of our hotel and even came right in wearing their big boots. Our mats were ruined in no time.

That's how I learned we had lost the war. We could hardly believe it. The Emperor was descended from the Sun Goddess, and our country had been fighting for him—surely the gods couldn't be defeated! But it had happened and everybody was terrified. All of Sakhalin became Russian property. The rest of Japan was occupied by the Americans, but it still belonged to us.

I watched as one after another of our friends and

relatives left with their few possessions for the big islands of Hokkaido or North Honshu. My father, home again after the war, decided early on to go with them. He collected the rest of the family together and departed. But Grandfather wasn't allowed to leave. He was head of the fire department and the Russians needed him. So we had to stay for another six months, but at last we were able to leave too. Life under the Russians was impossible. They had taken all our valuables, but Grandmother had managed to keep her diamond ring by turning it inwards. We could take only what we could carry, including a small rucksack with food in it, and everything else we possessed had to be left behind.

When we reached the ship, I didn't even want to go on board. It was dirty and we were crowded on the decks. When we did set off the sea tossed us backwards and forwards; there was no roof to protect us from sun or rain; food was scarce. All the children got terrible boils. It was like a nightmare. The grown-ups might have thought they were sailing to freedom, but I just thought life was getting worse and worse. I wanted to die, and I thought perhaps I was going to die.

And then we reached Hokkaido. What did it have for us?

CHAPTER FIVE

THE RED HANDBAG

WHEN we arrived in Hokkaido we joined my father and his second wife and my brothers and sisters. But we were all crowded together and food was scarce; so there were quarrels all the time. We travelled from place to place trying to make a living, and at last my grandparents separated from the rest of the family, taking me with them, and decided to set up a small shop.

Then I had to go to school. I hated it, and it was then that I began to long for a younger mother who would love me and really understand me. On parents' day Grandmother visited the school with the other mothers. My teacher complained about my low marks; I knew I would be scolded, and that it would make no difference. Grandmother was worried about me but she didn't know how to help. I was lonely and unhappy. And of course my bad temper and sulkiness didn't help me to make friends.

'Calf-neck! Calf-neck!' the boys would call out whenever I played outside. Stretch it as I might, I couldn't make my neck any longer. So I had to play indoors. I longed for toys and pretty things. Usually I got my own way, but if I didn't I would fly into a rage. Grandfather did his best for me, but there just wasn't any money to spare.

And then one day I got my chance. Some property had been sold, and for once there was a large amount of money in the house. Grandmother was out, and there in the drawer was her purse. I hesitated. It would be wrong to steal the money. Would anyone find out if I did? I could at least look and see how much there was inside—that wouldn't do any harm. I looked around cautiously . . . there was no one about. So I opened the purse. I had never seen so much money in my life! Stealthily I took out about £1—it wouldn't be missed from so much. How fortunate I was—how wonderful to have money I could spend!

Off I went to the shops to buy the pretty things I so much wanted. I quickly chose a bright red handbag, a mirror and some tree decorations. Then I realized that I couldn't show these prized possessions to anyone, because questions would be asked! I hid them in my room, but I was afraid every day of being found out. I felt guilty, and became more and more gloomy. Then one day Grandmother did discover them.

'Seiko, are these things yours?' she demanded. 'Where did you get them?'

'A rich friend lent them to me,' I lied.

'Then you must return them at once,' she insisted.

Now what could I do? I longed to hang on to them but didn't dare. Sadly I took them out of the house and went down to the river. I felt lonelier than ever as I watched the red handbag slowly disappear into the river. I had no friends and no toys; I was poor, a thief and a liar; and I had no real mother, only an old woman to look after me.

I managed to steal money once or twice more after that, and each time I felt less guilty. I always succeeded in getting a friend blamed for the losses and Grandmother believed what I told her.

It was about that time that I had a very nasty fright. My class was taken to a theatre to see slides of an old Buddhist story called *The Spider's Thread*.

A man who had been a rogue all his life spared the life of a spider one day instead of treading on it. It was the only good thing he had ever done. Then he

died, and was suffering agonies in the flames of hell. Suddenly above him he saw a spider making a long thread. It came lower and lower until it was within his grasp. Would it hold his weight? It was his only chance; he clutched at it and found that he could climb up this slender thread, out into paradise at the top. Yes, it was bearing his weight!

Then he looked down. Hundreds of other people were trying to cling to this thread to lift themselves out of torment. This was no good! The thread might break. Clinging on to it with his hands, he kicked back with his feet to throw the other climbers off. And as he did so he broke the thread and fell right back into the centre of the flames.

I listened, terrified. As I looked at that selfish man, I knew I was like him. I wanted my own way, I didn't care about anyone else, and I was a thief and a liar. Already I was in a hell of my own, and I didn't know how to escape. I didn't want to change, but I was scared. What was happening to me, and where would I go when I died? No one had ever told me about Jesus and his love. All I knew was fear.

CHAPTER SIX

THE DAY I PRAYED

GRANDFATHER was moving house once more, from Hokkaido to Honshu, the main island of Japan. It was a relief to be on the move again. This time the crossing by boat was lovely, with blue sea and mountains on either side. The ferry boat was crowded, but luxurious in comparison with the way we travelled when we left Sakhalin. Some people stretched out on the floor and went to sleep, but I found everything too interesting to go to sleep during the five-hour crossing to the mainland.

When we arrived in Honshu, we got on a little train with stoves in the carriages and chimneys through the windows. It chugged up the mountains past endless rice fields, taking us to our new home. I hoped this was going to be a new beginning, where the past could be forgotten.

But it didn't work out like that—life just got blacker and the guilt feeling stayed with me. I couldn't forget the stolen money and the red purse sinking in the river. I saw the spider's thread breaking.

My grandparents were growing older, and we were very poor. I didn't have enough food, and no pretty clothes. Grandmother spent more and more time clapping her hands and making long prayers at the god-shelf. Although we were such a long way from our first home, she still needed to inform the ancestors of what we were doing, and make sure she was offering them the right things. Every morning I knelt down with her and gave them a cup of water and some rice. I prayed that I might escape the tortures in the next world.

One day I looked at Grandfather and saw blood pouring from his nose. I was scared. He seemed to recover, but day after day the same thing happened. Then one night I was so worried I couldn't sleep. I prayed under the covers to the only gods I knew about —Grandmother's gods. I prayed that the bleeding would stop. It did!

Now I had the answer to all my problems! I must be quite sure to worship correctly every day and offer up rice and water. As a further discipline, I washed my face in cold water every morning, summer and winter alike. But although I did all these things faithfully, I was still unhappy.

Grandfather's business failed again. We had to move again, away from our beautiful mountain scenery and back to join my father on the north-east coast.

CHAPTER SEVEN

A GOOD IDEA

'CALF-NECK! Calf-neck! Funny-looking calf-neck!'

With the mocking voices of the boys ringing in my ears I ran home from school. I was desperate. What could I do? Where could I go? 'Home' was a wretched place, with the family quarrelling the whole time. Japan was recovering from the war; food and clothes were more plentiful and for most people life was getting easier. But for me it was nothing but darkness all the time.

My father's second wife was unpopular with everybody, and she knew that his frequent trips away from home weren't just for business. She knew she wasn't wanted, so she left. Soon after that he brought home his third wife.

Then my grandmother died. Once more a Buddhist

priest arrived in his black robe and began his dismal chanting. Incense sticks were burning all the time in front of the altar. I was careful to do all the right things: I prayed for her and helped to offer up fruit and flowers in front of the god-shelf. I wanted to help her in the spirit world, but I was also afraid in case I didn't worship correctly, and I would be punished after death —the spider's thread wouldn't hold me. But I loved Grandmother and was sorry when she died, although she'd always seemed old and unable to understand me. I felt more sorry for Grandfather, whom I loved very much.

My new 'mother', my father's third wife, was much younger, more like an older sister to me, and I soon had younger brothers. Somehow this just made me feel more lonely. The jeering and pointing of the boys at school infuriated me, and the more I lost my temper the more they teased. I hated going out of the house and I couldn't bear being sent shopping. As I grew up, I realized more and more how strange I looked—many people thought it was because I had done something wicked in a previous life. I had very few friends. So I decided there was only one thing left for me to do, and that was to work very hard at school. Up till now I'd always done badly, and I didn't care. Now I determined to do well, just to show that even a 'calf-neck' could hold a good head! My family was astonished when the next school report arrived, and I had a series of 'A's in every subject. At last I had achieved something, and I was very proud of myself. But I was still a lonely, sulky person.

I left the High School with credit, hoping that in the world outside I might find something different, some happiness, friendship, and justice.

CHAPTER EIGHT

HOPE

I was glad to leave school, and I hoped it would also be the end of all the teasing. 'What will it be like to work all day in an office?' I wondered. 'It will be good to be earning money, even if I have to hand most of it over to the family.'

The firm for which I worked was privately owned, most of the employees being members of the same family. At first I thought that would mean a friendly and helpful spirit, even though we had nothing but quarrels in my own family. But I was disappointed to find that the father of the family, the boss, was away most of the time, so the rest of the workers used every device they could think of to cheat and to get themselves more money. It wasn't really surprising, because the father was miserly and didn't pay them enough.

'Is the whole world like this?' I asked myself. 'Everybody trying to get as much as possible for himself, and not caring how much he hurts anyone else? Can't anybody be trusted? Is there any real love in the world?'

It was about that time that my eye happened to catch an advertisement in the local newspaper. It said that an Englishman was conducting an English Bible class free of charge. 'I'll go along and see what it's like,' I thought. I wasn't very interested in English although I'd studied it at school, and as for the Bible I didn't know anything about it at all. But it would be something to do.

I approached the building a little nervously, but the nervousness left me as soon as I got inside: there was such a friendly atmosphere in the meeting. I met Mr.

and Mrs. Fukuda and their daughter Yoko, and Yoko invited me to the Sunday evening Bible study meeting in their home.

I shall never forget her voice of welcome as she knelt at the porch of her home to greet me on my first visit. It was a small house, by no means wealthy. The family could have been quite well off if the father hadn't wasted his money and his life on drink. Perhaps that was why Mrs. Fukuda looked so thin and strained. But her welcome to me was warm and real. Each time I went to the house she welcomed me like her own daughter. Yoko and I were about the same age, and she treated me as a friend. There was a peacefulness there I had never met before, which was a complete contrast to the tension and quarrelling at home. I liked the hymn singing as we sat around the room on cushions. We prayed to a heavenly Father who had created the world; but there was no god-shelf in the room and no idol to worship. They just closed their eyes and spoke to Jesus as though He was there. I longed for the joy I heard about and could see on the faces of the Christians. But when I went home there was a struggle in my heart. I wanted to become a Christian, but there were many things I couldn't understand, and I didn't want to give up my right to please myself. I was on the spider's thread, but kicking.

A few weeks later I had to have an operation on my nose, and when I came out of hospital I couldn't speak very well and felt embarrassed. So once more I didn't go out if I could help it. I stopped going to Yoko's house, and the Christian meetings too. By the time I was better I had got out of the habit of going. I thought about the church, the warmth of the Fukudas' welcome and the peace in the meetings, but I didn't really want to go back. I couldn't really believe it was for me that Christ had died.

CHAPTER NINE

JOY

ONE evening on my way home from work, I was waiting at the bus stop when I saw two men striding along the road in my direction. Soon I could see that they were foreigners, and I recognized the missionary and his friend. I was ashamed to meet them because I had been away from the meeting so long, so I hid behind some other people. The missionaries stopped to look at the bus timetable. To my relief they were engrossed in conversation and went on without noticing me. But seeing them had made me want to go back to the meetings again.

The following night I was there at the Bible study meeting, enjoying the atmosphere and Yoko's friendship.

'It's good to see you again,' she greeted me. 'We've missed you!'

'I stopped coming when I had to have an operation on my nose,' I excused myself. 'I couldn't speak properly for some time.'

'I'm sorry about that,' said Yoko. 'I hope you are really better. We've been praying for you—we were worried about you.'

This concern touched me, because no one had cared about me before. This kind of love was something I'd lacked all my life. As I left she handed me a book, saying, 'I think you'd be interested in this story. It's about a missionary to China, written by a Chinese and translated into Japanese.'

The book was the life story of Hudson Taylor. I took it home and it spoke to me about a living God who cared for men. It mattered to Him what we did.

31

It seemed as though the way I had been worshipping at the god-shelf and making offerings to my ancestors, the only religion I had known, was wrong. Slowly I began to realize how sinful I was. This was quite different from the sense of fear I had had when I heard the story of the spider's thread. Gradually I understood that there was only one true God and that Jesus Christ His Son had lived on this earth to tell us about Him.

Soon after this a friend invited me to some special Christian meetings, and I heard again about the love of Jesus in dying on a cruel cross for me. I heard that He was willing to forgive my sins, to come into my heart and to live with me day by day. I was drawn to Christ that night, specially to His love. Love was something for which I longed and it was too wonderful to think that God should love me. When the speaker invited us to put our trust in Christ and give our lives to Him, I couldn't do anything else: I raised my hand to show my decision.

My missionary friend had been present when I went forward to show I had trusted Christ as my Saviour. 'This is wonderful!' he exclaimed afterwards. 'Will you tell everyone in church next Sunday? Just say how you came to trust Him as your Saviour and what difference it is making to you.'

On Sunday I began very nervously, but I knew God Himself had given me faith. I knew He was real. I was sure He had saved me. And as I spoke joy flooded my heart. JOY! This was wonderfully new. I forgot my problems, my neck, my sorrows, myself. Even the spider's thread terrified me no longer. I was out of hell and up in the sunshine. I couldn't help smiling. 'In your presence is fulness of joy,' it says in

the Psalms. I had something I had been longing for, had hardly believed possible: first love and now joy. I wanted to share it with everybody. I knew I would have to follow Jesus wherever He led me, and that was what I wanted to do.

I didn't suspect the trouble that was coming, but I would have gone ahead even if I had known.

CHAPTER TEN

THE OUTCAST

THINGS changed very quickly after that. I had never been really happy with the firm I was working for. There was constant quarrelling and dishonesty. I had to keep two sets of books—the real accounts, and another set to show to tax officials. Now that I belonged to Christ I couldn't do that any longer.

I talked it over with my father.

'What are you so worried about?' he asked. 'Everybody does that. They couldn't run a business without it.'

'But now I belong to Christ I can't cheat, Father.'

'You'd better forget that sort of rubbish!' he replied angrily. But, because he could see I was unhappy, he eventually agreed, 'Do what you think is best'.

The next day I resigned. I had no idea what lay ahead, but a wonderful joy filled my heart. I knew my Lord was pleased. I stayed at home praying that He would show me what to do. But Mother was very annoyed. 'You're a stupid good-for-nothing girl!' she scolded. 'Do you expect people to look after you all your life? Why don't you go out to work?'

'I'm asking Jesus to guide me,' I answered. 'I must do what he wants and not be dishonest.'

'Jesus! Who's he, anyway? Some foreign god? You'd do better following the ways of your ancestors instead of talking about a god you can't even see. At least you could go to the labour exchange and try to find a job.'

I stayed at home for a month, but finally I realized it was wrong just to live there without paying for my keep. So one morning I set off for the labour exchange praying, 'Lord, if I'm offered work, show me whether or not it is your will for me'. I sat down to wait my turn, and as I began reading my Bible the words 'I will make you fishers of men' leaped out of the page. I knew they were for me, from God, but I couldn't understand what He was trying to say to me.

There wasn't any work for me, and I was told to return the next day. Quickly I left the building to accompany the missionary on a hospital visit, as I had promised.

'Good morning, Seiko San,' he greeted me. 'Did you get a job?'

'No,' I answered. 'They told me to go back tomorrow.'

'My wife and I have been praying for you, and asking the Lord to give you Bible training. What do you think about it? Would you like us to get details of Bible schools for you?'

Then I realized what 'Fishers of men' meant. I said simply, 'Yes please'.

When I reached home, I said nothing about the Bible school. I didn't even have any money from the labour exchange, because I had told them about the odd jobs I'd been doing. Father was furious. 'No one in their right mind would declare that small amount! Are you crazy? Even the labour exchange wouldn't expect you to.'

I couldn't get into the three Bible schools the missionary contacted for me. Then I remembered seeing an advertisement in a Christian magazine, offering free Bible training in the mornings for those who would work teaching children in the afternoons. I passed the exam and was invited to join.

When I told my family what I had done, there was

a terrific uproar. The whole family met in conference to decide what to do about me. I had told Grandfather, who was getting old and frail, a little about my Lord, but even he was against my new faith. I didn't want to hurt him, I just wanted him to know Christ too. Father's temper had been roused over much smaller things than this, and I knew I couldn't expect any sympathy now. He pronounced the final verdict next morning.

'You're a pig-headed, ungrateful girl. Go to Bible school if you must, but don't consider yourself part of the family any more, and don't dare to return here again.'

But the day before I left Mother prepared special food, and the next day Father said quietly, 'If you are sick, come right back home'. I left in tears with one small suitcase, but in my heart I had a deep peace from God.

CHAPTER ELEVEN

GRANDFATHER

THE 'Bible School' that year had only two students. We studied in the mornings and had different kinds of meetings in the afternoons. I learned to speak at children's meetings, and I specially loved doing that. As I looked into the faces of the boys and girls, I wished somebody had told me about Jesus when I was their age. I spoke in tents too, and learned how to lead meetings. But after a year I still wasn't satisfied. I wanted to learn more.

God told me He would do something better for me, and about that time I met the principal of the new Hokkaido Bible Institute. As I talked to him I felt sure that that was the place for me.

On my way to the northern island of Hokkaido, I was able to call in at my home, because my father's fury had subsided a little. It was good to talk to Grand-father again. He was ageing rapidly. I told him simply how Jesus had died for him so that if he trusted Him his sins would be forgiven and he would go to heaven.

'No, Seiko,' he answered slowly. 'That's too simple. I hope I have done enough good in my life, but I don't know.'

Ten days later he had a stroke and was in a coma for three days. The doctor told us we should prepare for the funeral.

I was alone in the house with him when the doctor called to give him an injection. He warned me that he would probably never open his eyes again.

'Lord,' I prayed, 'Grandfather doesn't know You. He isn't saved. I was able to tell him a little bit about

You before, but not enough. Please, please don't let him die without your salvation.'

I sat on the floor by his bed, thinking about the past, remembering the happy times with Grandfather, who meant more to me than any other human being. I couldn't bear him to die and go to hell. Slowly his breathing improved, and he opened his eyes and looked at me. He couldn't speak, but he could understand what I said. Over the next few days I told him again about the Lord Jesus, in simple words as though I were talking to a small child.

'Do you want to go to heaven, Grandfather?' I asked.

'Mm!' he murmured, meaning 'Yes!'

'I can tell you how,' I said, and bit by bit I told him as much as he could take in. 'God loves you. Jesus died on a cross for you. He rose from the dead. He is stronger than death and hell.'

'Mm!' Grandfather showed that he could understand.

'Will you trust Him to save you and take you there?'

'Mm! Mm!' Grandfather grunted again.

Slowly he seemed to get it all. Although his speech hadn't returned I could tell he was trusting Jesus. I felt so happy and thankful.

His condition improved. One day when he was in a happy mood I said to him, 'How wonderful that you are well again! Jesus has healed you. He not only heals bodies but can forgive your sins as well.'

With happy tears Grandfather replied, 'It's wonderful, wonderful'.

The next time the doctor called he was amazed to see Grandfather. 'I gave him an injection,' he stated, 'but this improvement isn't due to it. Something wonderful has happened.'

It was during my first year at Hokkaido Bible Institute that my grandfather finally went to be with the Lord. Two weeks previously my missionary friend had visited him. He was so ill that my step-mother hadn't wanted her to come in.

'I promised Seiko I would visit him,' she pleaded. 'How can I face her if I don't see her beloved grandfather.'

With this my step-mother took her into the back room where Grandfather was lying, with the quilt over the charcoal stove as well as his body to keep him warm. My friend talked a little about the Lord. He understood. Then she suggested that they should pray. He tried to get up but she assured him it was quite all right to pray lying down. She felt sure that the Lord Himself was with them and that Grandfather was ready to meet Him.

As she left she turned to my step-mother. 'It's wonderful to know that he's trusting in Christ. There's no fear for him now. Seiko will be relieved. It's the thing we long for most for those we love.'

When I received a telegram telling me to return home because he was critically ill, I knew as I boarded the train that I wouldn't see him alive again. I was happy that I would see him one day in heaven.

The funeral service was difficult. I couldn't offer up incense or food at the god-shelf, now that I belonged to Christ—I couldn't follow the Buddhist practices. I knew that there was no need to pray for or to Grandfather now. I wanted to tell all the guests at the funeral about my Saviour and his, and so I gave them tracts.

Again my father was furious. 'If you can't behave like any sensible human being you'd better stay well away from home,' he shouted. 'You've brought shame on the family!'

CHAPTER TWELVE

THE LIGHT OF THE WORLD

AFTER three years at the Hokkaido Bible Institute I came back to my own county, so I can visit my family sometimes. I work for the Light of the World gospel broadcasts, and my job is to answer letters from listeners who hear about Jesus over the radio and want to know more. Often they write to me and say how lonely they are, because they have no friends. I write back and say,

'I know exactly how you feel. I was like that until Jesus came into my heart. Now I have His friendship and joy.' It is wonderful to be able to tell people about Him.

There are boys in a reform school—there because the police have caught them breaking the law. Sometimes I get letters from them. They write about their problems, and I think back to the days when the story of the spider's thread scared me so. Then I can tell them of a Saviour who forgives sins and helps us to live victorious lives. It is lovely to get replies like:

'I have found while I have been here that Christ does indeed give me power to do the right thing.'

Sometimes patients from hospital write to me. They often think that they are sick because they have done something wrong and are being punished. I write and tell them that I had the same worries because of my funny neck. They can find hope in Christ.

Sometimes I get letters from people who live miles away from any church or Christians. I am so thankful that they can hear of my Lord through the radio broadcast.

Sometimes I am specially happy when children write to me—children like Takako San. She's a ten-year-old who's been studying the Bible by correspondence and has come to trust in Jesus. She's been taking a dozen friends to Sunday School with her, and teaching others who can't go. She's really happy. I wish I'd heard about Jesus when I was her age—then I wouldn't have spent so long praying to idols or to the dead. I wouldn't have washed in cold water in winter. I wouldn't have been terrified of death and the Buddhist hell. I would have known joy.

I wonder who will be the next person to write to me, who will find real joy in the Lord Jesus?